Since 2020

Written, Created and Edited by Paul Doherty

Photography by the Stance Auto Media Team

and Independent Photographers.

Enrique Munoz

1997 Toyota Supra Turbo
Instagram: @kingerm_supra
Photographer: @mr2mivin

6

Theo August

2003 Nissan 350z Japan import
Instagram: @theosbook
Photographer: @incogmedia

16

Zac Ganfield

2009 Mk2 Ford Focus RS
Instagram: @thatgymkhanarep
Photographer: k.k photography by Katie

30

Ethan Herman.

2012 Subaru Impreza WRX STI
Instagram: @_nxflash_

40

Eric Strickland

1995 Nissan Skyline BCNR33
Instagram: @okiegtr
Photographer: @oadam7
Photographer: @ulphotog

44

This is our Monthly Magazine, Real life stories from all over the world, Groups and Clubs that may interest you, and some of the best Photography from some very talented photographers. All these stories are from the actual owners of the cars, their life in the car street scene, what inspires them and some handy tips and advice for anyone thinking of buying the same car, we hope that you get some inspiration from people just like you building their dream cars, although we have corrected most of the Grammar and Spelling mistakes we feel we should leave some as these stories are straight from the owners, their own words.

We invite everyone with a high spec or modified car to submit their cars and story to feature in this magazine and also our Online MAG, why don't you come along and join us in our Facebook group and get to know us and some of the owners, ask questions and submit your own car, you'll find we are all very friendly, this is a community for us all.

We also have Calendars, Hoodies, T-shirts, Magazines and Stickers available from our Store
Merchandise Store: stanceautomag.com and Etsy just search Stance Auto Magazine
To follow us, submit your car or join us check out our Links
Instagram:@stanceautomag
Facebook: @stanceautomag
Submit Your Car and Story: https://stanceauto.co.uk/submissions/

Jeff Perez
1991 Nissan Skyline GTR

Instagram: @bnr32.jp

Photographer: @mr2mivin

My name is Jeff Perez and I'm 36 years old, I worked at General Motors dealerships as a technician when I was younger but have been working in Oil Refineries for the last 15 years.

So I decided to Customize the Car, it all started with just the GReddy intake kit with the Airinix filters.

Then I came across a great deal on a set of GReddy T517Z twin turbos, (I wanted to keep it twins) and from there it just spiralled into a full build.

As time went on I went with mostly all GReddy parts so it got to a point where it became the theme.

It's based on the OG GReddy RX of the '90s and the car has many old TRUST parts that have been discontinued for decades.

Owning and driving a Skyline in the USA is definitely quite the experience, it does get a lot of attention.

The way it sounds makes you feel like you are Brian O'Connor in 2 Fast 2 Furious!!

At times it is overwhelming because I can go to a meet where there are million-dollar cars and my Nissan is attracting more attention.

At the same time though there is a good community of Skyline owners and everyone seems to know each other somehow. I've made friends by meeting them at car shows, even from selling parts to one another.

Advice/Tips?

There are always going to be haters no matter how you build your car so just make it your own.

As long as you are happy with how you are doing the build that's all that matters. Do it for yourself not the clout.

Now working on my cars is purely a hobby and I have met a lot of cool people in the industry from going to car shows and meets.

My very first interests were from TV shows like Knight Rider and Dukes of Hazard. I was initially all about American Muscle! My first car was a black 84 Fire bird and it looked just like Knight Rider.

Once I got that car the rest was history, I was hooked. I have now had several cars from many different makes. Once I started going to car shows and meets I made a lot of friends through the car community.

There is a very good car culture out here in Southern California.

Originally I actually really wanted an R33 GTR, the one that everyone hates haha. But here in the USA, there is a 25-year rule for imports so I would have had to wait several years to get one.

While continuing to go to meets I began to see R32 GTR's as they hit the 25-year mark and the more I saw them the more I started to like them. Before I knew it, the R32 had become my favourite of them all.

When I found my car it had only 35,000 km and It was completely stock!!!!

I did all of the work myself, except when it was necessary for more than one person, I had friends there to help.

It has really been a great experience because this was the first turbo car I've owned so I have learned so much about this type of build and making it my own. With tuner cars no two are the same, that's for sure

Future Plans:

I actually have a set of GREX Alcon brakes that I have been wanting to put on. There were fitment issues so the next project is making them work. They are much bigger and will give much more stopping power.

What does the car scene mean to me, I have met a lot of good people within the car community, no matter what your race is or where you come from we have the same interests. I also get satisfaction from the way so many people give back. I go to a lot of charity car shows where they collect for toy drives or products for school children and it really makes a difference.

Dream car:

At this point in my life, I would like to go back to where it all started and do a complete Knight Rider build. It would have the red scanner on the front, full talking dash with the crazy interior!!!! It would stand out at a show too that's for sure.

Spec List

Engine:
- †– GReddy T517Z twin turbos
- †– TRUST GREX oil filter relocation kit with oil cooler
- †– GReddy oil filter
- †– GReddy suction kit with Airinix filters
- †– TRUST inter-cooler with GReddy piping
- †– GReddy radiator
- †– GReddy aluminium radiator top pipe
- †– GReddy breather tank with GReddy 36mm adaptor
- †– GReddy FV-2 blow off valve
- †– GReddy fuel rail
- †– GReddy catch can
- †– GReddy oil cap
- †– GReddy RB26 Engine Ornament
- †– Vacuum manifold block ran with blue GReddy vacuum lines
- †– Haltech Elite 2000 ECU
- †– Spitfire Coil-packs
- †– Tomei fuel pressure regulator
- †– AEM 320 LPH fuel pump
- †– Injector Dynamics ID1000 injectors

Exhaust:
- †– TRUST down-pipe
- †– TRUST PE-TiR exhaust

Interior:
- †– TRUST steering wheel
- †– GReddy steering wheel bolts
- †– GReddy/WB steering wheel quick release and lock
- †– TRUST racing harnesses and shoulder pads
- †– TRUST GREX shift knob with GReddy carbon cover
- †– GReddy shift boot and hand brake boot
- †– GReddy Infometer Touch
- †– GReddy skeleton blue turbo timer
- †– Tablet display operating via Haltech
- †– Nismo white face cluster and sub-meter gauges

Exterior:
- †– GReddy GRacer front bumper
- †– GReddy GRacer side skirts
- †– GReddy GRacer rear spats
- †– GReddy GRacer adjustable rear spoiler
- †– GReddy RX graphics
- †– Japsalon J-Tune hood (bonnet) with AeroCatch pins
- †– GK Tech aero mirrors

Wheels:
- †– Panasport G7 C5C2 17x9.5

Suspension:
- †– HKS Hipermax lV coilovers
- †– Nismo front and rear tower bars
- †– Do-Luck crossbar

Brakes:
- †– Stock GTR brakes

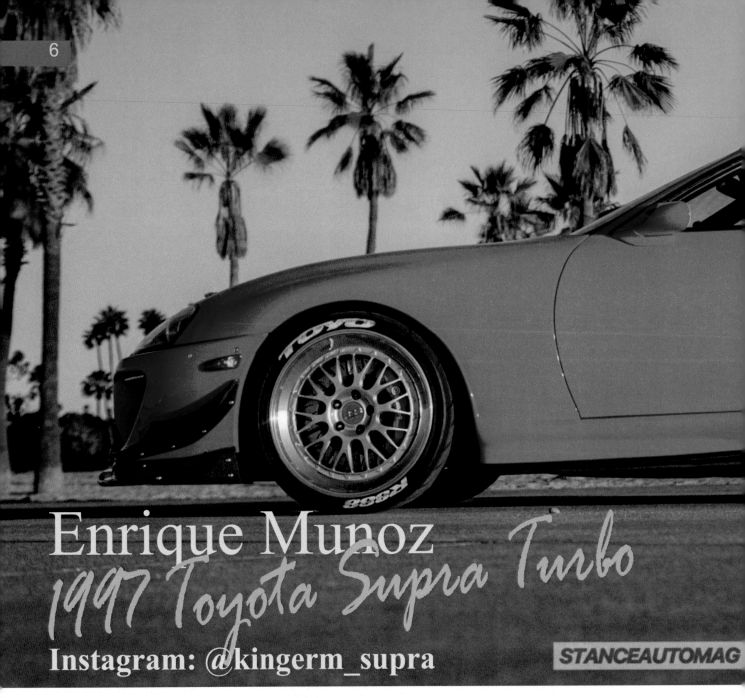

Enrique Munoz
1997 Toyota Supra Turbo
Instagram: @kingerm_supra

STANCEAUTOMAG

My name is Enrique Munoz. I'm born and raised in sunny Los Angeles, CA. The epicentre of JDM car culture.

I currently work in the video game industry. I make cinematics for the games you love to play. Previous to this I worked on Film & Television doing Visual F/X for blockbuster movies and TV shows.

In my spare time, I like checking out cool cars at meets, attending Racecar Events and enjoy watching MMA either live or however possible.

My fascination with Supra's started back when I was in high school in the early/mid-'90s. A friend of mine had a JGTC (Japan Grand Touring Championship) poster with 2 Supra's battling it out which I loved. At the same time, there were street races that happened on Sunday nights in Long Beach.

This is where I came across a Royal Sapphire Blue coloured Supra that left me awestruck. It destroyed everything it went up against. I was sold! It wasn't until 2001 when I found the perfect example on toyotacertified.com no less (now defunct website).

That very same moment I called the dealership (in Mars, PA of all places...) and put a deposit with my credit card. I flew out that same night and bought the car the very next day.

Little did I know that this 1 decision would help shape the rest of my life.Back in the '90s, Japanese cars were not known for going fast in the quarter-mile.

The same friend with the poster had magazine subscriptions to all the car magazines at the time. One of these magazines had on the cover a Supra that had just broken the 10-second quarter-mile record for ANY Japanese car.

This immediately piqued my interest and I read about the guys behind the magic. It was drag racing legend Vinny Ten (ironically enough, with a name "Ten") and two twin brothers from Queens NY, Marc and Eric Kozeluh.

From then on I fantasized about having these guys working on my car but with them being on the other side of the country it all seemed like a pipe dream.

Flash forward a couple of years and I'm enjoying my car, driving it around town and taking it to the occasional track day. The bug to start modifying the car was too great.

Being an artist by trade gave me the excuse to change the look of the car with aftermarket aero. This would lead me to Japan for the Tokyo Auto Salon 2003 while on a tour with now-defunct Turbo magazine.

At the show I made it a mission to meet racing star Manabu 'Max' Orido, then owner of Ridox brand Supra Bodykit.

ARVIN RECINOS   Photographer   Marvin Recinos - @mr2mivin

This kit, being designed by a racecar driver in the JGTC, had the JGTC look I had fallen in love with years earlier.

Being the first one to import this from Japan into the USA it was neither easy nor cheap but I got the lawyer (customs), paid the air freight, and import fees to make it all happen.

I got the car all put back together now in a different shade of red (now "Rossa Corsa" from Toyota's "Renaissance Red") and she looked awesome.

I still had so much more to do especially mechanically, little did I know at the time how long it would take to get to this aspect of the build.

I was extremely happy with the car and its build progress but with anything in life, other things can get in the way. In 2004 I bought a house and my financial commitments were on everything but the car. The car sat for years. With all, I had done it was in a state that it was not easy to drive or just use as a normal car.

It got so little use I contemplated selling the car in 2007. After talking with family and friends and them stressing me to not sell, it wasn't until I spoke with my mom and she of all people (she didn't like that I had a fast sports car for my safety) convinced me to keep it, and so it sat.

As fate would have it, during this time Eric and Marc Kozeluh - the twin brothers from New York, had moved out to the West Coast in sunny Long Beach. Now known as Twins Turbo Motorsports – the shop responsible for building Vaughn Gittin Jr.'s RTR-X Mustang and the twin Turbo Viper that appears in the Need for Speed video game as the final boss car, along with many other radical street and track cars.

I knew they were the only shop that could work on my car.I met with the Twins in 2010 and after our meeting, I had a reality check of the price and extent of the kind of build I had envisioned.

I left with a 3-page laundry list of parts that would be needed and a greater understanding of what it was going to take to make it happen (money and lots of it!), a complete rebuild from the ground up.

I didn't give up, for the next 2 years I saved up and sourced parts from the list and stockpiled them for the day I would be able to return to the Twins.

Once the faithful day did arrive, early 2012, the Twins were impressed with my perseverance and this was the spark that would lead to our synergistic mash-up, them with the engineering expertise and me with my artist background.

What follows is a build to rival any car build let alone a Supra. What could be so special about a Supra with a single turbo conversion?

One look at the engine bay and you'll realize this is anything but your typical bolt-on parts build. Everything in the engine bay is hand finished metal.

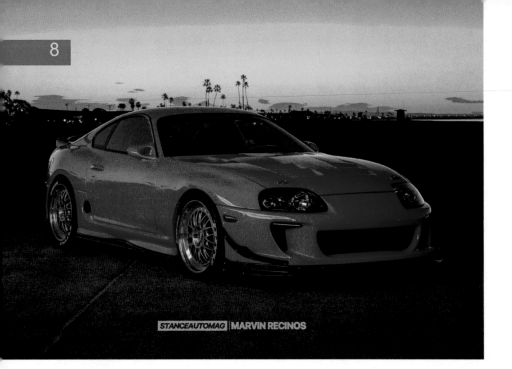

STANCEAUTOMAG | MARVIN RECINOS

We took great influence from the hotrod scene and went for a "clean look". Minimal wires, cables, everything!

A new custom harness was crafted, bespoke parts were made like the intercooler with its hand-hammered end tanks, the front of the engine bay was completely remodelled to accommodate the v-mount intercooler/radiator setup and all the custom ducting under the front bumper.

All the parts were converted to metric (some parts like the intake manifold came from Australia, imperial measurement), all bolts where possible were converted to an ARP stud and 12-star nut combo.

The whole underside was stripped to the bone so to speak, bare metal. All undercarriage bolts (and engine bay bolts not replaced with ARP) were shipped to be cadmium plated (40-pound box!).

Custom BBS Motorsport wheels, custom LED lighting, Brembo monobloc brakes with custom colour match paint, are just a few of the many top-shelf and bespoke parts that helped make this car what it is.Taking the hotrod theme to heart, who else to work on the interior but the shop from the TV show, **American Hotrod**.

Enter Gabe's Street Rod Custom Interiors. The whole interior is wrapped in leather with red stitching. Even the roll cage is hand-sewn wrapped in leather.

When you open the door to the car it still smells like a woman's purse store! Little details you may miss, the Recaro seats are covered in woven leather, a true weave not a print.

I was able to source vintage Recaro badges from a 1970's Ford Cosworth.

When I first started building the car with the Twins the build was such a radical departure from any other Supra build I actually thought other Supra owners would hate it and shun me (I being in Southern California, there are plenty of Supra owners and we all know each other).

Little did I know the reception it would receive once it was unveiled at the Supra National meet, Supras in Vegas 2014. It would go on to grace the cover of SuperStreet magazine twice (within 1 year), go to SEMA and compete in the Battle of Builders 2015 and break into the Top 10, a first for a Japanese car to be alongside and recognized with such builders as Chip Foose, the Ring Brothers, and Bobby Alloway.

It recently completed a tenure at the Petersen Automotive Museum as part of the

"World Tour"

in their Vault collection.

As great as these accolades are, the one true thing this car has given me is to show me what it means to stay committed and push through when it gets hard and see something to completion.

This car and the build oddly enough helped me grow up and helped me commit to my now wife. Previous to building the car, in my life when things got tough. I would abandon them or just never see anything to completion either out of fear or not being brave enough to push through that last 10% that always seems to come up just before excellence.

This build showed that with hard work, and a commitment to finish what can be waiting for you at the end of the struggle, the hustle, the grind.

Completing the build helped mature me to where I wanted to marry my long time girlfriend and now wife. This car changed my life in every way. At the end of the day, these cars are all about the people behind them. As much as this car is a reflection of me, I in my present-day reflect the car.

It also reflects on the talents and skills of all the people who helped make my car what it is today. I will forever be grateful to them for making my dream car a reality.

Advice/Tips

Build your car for you. Don't follow trends. Don't do as others do or say. If it so happens that it falls with what you're thinking and wanting to do, then so be it. But the biggest piece of advice I could say is to make sure you build your car for yourself.

SPEC LIST

ENGINE
- † Toyota 2JZ-GTE,
- † Precision 6766 turbo,
- † Full-Race T4 divided header and 4-inch downpipe,
- † Custom V-mount setup with Bell intercooler core & hand-hammered end tanks,
- † HKS 264 cams,
- † Adjustable cam gears,
- † HyperTune intake and 90mm throttle body,
- † Accufab clamps on custom TT intercooler pipes,
- † Custom dual-pass C+R radiator,
- † Setrab oil cooler & power steering cooler,
- † ID2000 injectors,
- † Twins Turbo HyperTune cable bracket,
- † Twins Turbo MK4 short throttle cable,
- † Twins Turbo thermostat housing rotator kit,
- † Twins Turbo Inconel T4 divided turbo inlet gasket,
- † Twins Turbo Inconel turbine heat shield,
- † Brown & Miller hose & crimp fittings,
- † 4-inch stainless steel oval exhaust tubing with 4-inch electric exhaust cut-out from mid-pipe,
- † Veilside Ti muffler, 2x Bosch 044 fuel pumps with flex-fuel sensor for E85,
- † -10/-8 stainless steel fuel feed & return hard lines,
- † Weldon fuel pressure regulator,
- † Weldon fuel filters,
- † MoTeC M820 engine management system with a custom harness

STANCEAUTOMAG | MARVIN RECINOS

STANCEAUTOMAG | MARVIN RECINOS

STANCEAUTOMAG | MARVIN RECINOS

STANCEAUTOMAG | MARVIN RECINOS

SUSPENSION/BRAKES

- †– HKS Hipermax Max IV GT coilovers,
- †– TRD sway bars, Brembo 6-piston calipers (front),
- †– 4-piston calipers (rear) custom painted to match the body colour,
- †– Brembo slotted/vented 2-piece rotors

WHEELS/TIRES

- †– BBS Motorsport E88 wheels (custom size) 19×10.5-inch (front) 19×11.5-inch (rear),
- †– Toyo R888 tires 265/30/19 (front) 305/30/19 (rear),
- †– Custom-plated ARP wheel studs

EXTERIOR

- †– Custom metalwork and ducting,
- †– Ridox front bumper carbon fibre,
- †– Ridox front splitter carbon fibre,
- †– Ridox front canards carbon fibre,
- †– Ridox wide front fenders FRP,
- †– Ridox side skirts carbon fibre,
- †– Ridox rear skirts carbon fibre,
- †– Ridox trunk lip wing carbon fibre,
- †– Ridox GT wing,
- †– Top Secret hood carbon fibre,
- †– Top Secret diffuser carbon fibre,
- †– Ganador side mirrors carbon fibre,
- †– Custom LED bars for turn signals,
- †– Paint color Ferrari Rosso Corsa

INTERIOR

- †– Full leather-wrapped interior with hand-sewn custom Chromoly 6-point roll cage,
- †– TRD Tachometer,
- †– TRD Steering Wheel,
- †– Recaro sport seats in black and red leather stitching with real woven leather customized with vintage 70's Recaro badging,
- †– Custom seat mounts,
- †– Custom LED instrument setup by Stu Hagen,
- †– Veilside pedals and shift knob,
- †– Carbon fibre steering column (Whifbitz)
- †– Masterminds behind the whole build, fabrication - Twins Turbo Motorsports
- †– Engine bay metal work - Mark Delong
- †– Paint/Bodywork - Buddha Concept Designs
- †– Electronics/Harness - Greg Pyle
- †– Tuning - Shane Tecklenburg
- †– Interior - Gabe's Street Rod Custom Interiors

DRIVELINE

- †– Factory Getrag 6-speed transmission,
- †– Tilton CC triple-plate clutch,
- †– Remote shaft-mounted slave cylinder with Twins Turbo clutch master cylinder kit,
- †– TRD LSD

STANCEAUTOMAG | MARVIN RECINOS

My name is Larry Flores, I'm from Corpus Christi. TX. I've had a project or project since I was 15.

Earlier if you count BMX bikes, lol. I got a job when I was 15 (lied about my age) because I wanted to buy a car that my stepdad was selling. I had a choice between a 1975 Datsun 280z or a 1980 Volkswagen Scirocco.

This was 1988, so both were pretty used and needed work. I was drawn to the Datsun more than the Volkswagen and that's what I ended up with. I think that was the best thing for me, to own a car that needed a lot of attention, or I wasn't going anywhere.

Growing up, my dad had several different cars, but one car that I always remembered was my favourite one. He had a 1971 Datsun 240z, I guess that explains the draw to the 280z. Fast forward a bit, got older, had a family now and working on a career, so my project time was very limited. I ended up buying another 280z, a 1978 this time.

Now that I had a bit more experience and little more cash than I had 20 years prior I was ready to do a lot of the things to the '78 that I had wanted to do to the '75. I wanted it to be better than stock, kind of always been that way.

An LS swap was a consideration, but I really liked upgrading with parts from the same family. So, I decided to go with an L28ET upgrade for the Z to keep it in the Datsun/Nissan family.

That's what kind of brought me or helped me find my direction to a 1987 R10 that I have now. I was still interested in LS swapping something. I was very intrigued by what everyone was doing with this platform, and I wanted to do something as well. I knew finding the right Chevy wouldn't be hard.

All the older Chevy's have always caught my eye. But there was just something about old Chevy trucks that I just loved, especially the Squarebodies. So, I decided that would be my next project.

My first attempt was a 1986 Chevy Short-bed Utility Truck. I had this truck for 6 months. Very clean California rust free truck. Unfortunately, it was stolen from where I worked.

Larry Flores
1987 Chevy R10

Photographer: Adam Delgadillo - @oadam7

We had a 5-acre yard that I kept it in. The second attempt was a 1969 C10 Step Side. Started moving quickly on this one. I found a 6.2/6L80 set up for it, started ordering motor mounts, cross member, suspension, brake parts, plug and play wiring harness and custom wheels for it.

I was doing all this while still looking to see if I could find a good deal on another Squarebody. Well, seek and ye shall find. I found another square that was in really good shape, and I just couldn't pass it up. So, I quickly pumped the brakes on the '69 and

I decided to rebuild the 6.2, so I took it to a friend of mine Martin Corona/ Sinton, TX. Everyone knows an LS guy, that's my LS guy.

Complete tear down and rebuild heads getting worked on and block sent to the machine shop.

We figured now that it's opened let's change a few things to make it better. (better = faster).

LS7 lifters, springs, pushrods and Texas Speed stage 3 cam. Did the variable valve timing delete, no need for 4 cylinder mode?

AUTOMAG | ADAM DELGADILLO

The motor was back together quickly, we had some fuel tank and wiring issues to sort out and once that was done it was ready to fire up and it did.

"Sounded amazing with a base tune and open headers"!

Once I got the exhaust worked on, I went to Unlimited Performance so Rick could get it tuned. It ran awesome after that. Next up, was the suspension, brakes and the custom wheels I ordered needed to be put on.

I had to do a 5 lug to 6 lug conversion since these wheels were ordered for the '69 I was previously working on. I took it to Viet Automotive, Tim Viet took care of me there.

We decided on doing a 4-link coil-over suspension set up for the rear, it needed to be tubed and C-notched, the rear end was rebuilt to handle the extra horsepower as well. I went with Wilwood brakes front and rear and just a drop spindle and drop springs and shocks for the front. Once the motor and suspension were dialled in it was off to the paint shop.

Jacob Compton @AfterHoursCustomsCC really knocked it out of the park. I told him what I wanted, and he executed it flawlessly. Excellent work!! I wanted a colour scheme that you don't see very often on these trucks and that is exactly what I got.

Overall, I loved the experiences that come with doing projects like these.

During the process, you get to meet a lot of cool people that are doing some very cool things, an easy way to get motivated.

Not sure what the next project will be, but I have two boys that are 13 and 14, so I'm more than sure something will come up.

STANCEAUTOMAG ADAM DELGADILLO

STANCEAUTOMAG ADAM DELGADILLO

STANCEAUTOMAG ADAM DELGADILLO

SPEC LIST

† – Engine from a 2008 Escalade Gen IV 6.2/6l80 combo
† – Texas Speed Stage 3 Cam - 273/277
† – Ported/Polished Heads
† – LS7 Push Rods and New springs
† – Variable Valve Timing Delete
† – Texas Speed Long Tube Headers
† – Tejas Steel Motor Mounts and Cross member
† – Melling Oil Pump
† – Painless Performance Wire Harness
† – Ron Francis Dual Fan Wiring Harness
† – Derale Performance High Output Dual 13" Fan set up
† – Holly Sniper In-Tank Fuel Pump
† – 10 Bolt Rear Custom Quick Performance Axels with a Mini Spool, 373 Gears
† – Quick Performance 4 Link Kit with CCP Rear Coil-Over set up.
† – Wilwood Brakes Front and Rear from Little Shop Manufacturing
† – Shorten Rear End by 5" and C-Clip Eliminators installed
† – 2.5 Drop Spindles with 3" CCP Drop Springs for the Front
† – 5 lug to 6 lug conversion
† – Custom Made Intro Wheels, originally designed for a 5 spoke wheel but made into a 6 spoke
† – 20 x 15 Rear and 20 x 9 .5 Front
† – Wrapped with Mickey Thompson Sportsman S/R's Front 245/45R -20 and Rear 29.0 x 15OR-20LT
† – 3" Dual Exhaust with (2) 40 Series Flowmasters
† – Dakota Digital RTX Gauges
† – Forever Sharp Steering Wheel
† – Pioneer DEH-P9400BH Head Unit
† – Factory Heat and Air-condition

Paint and Bodywork were done by Jacob Compton @AfterHoursCustomsCC
Tuned by Rick @UnlimitedPerformance
Re-built Rear End, Brakes & Suspension Work by Tim Veit @VeitAutomotive
Motor Re-built by Martin Corona/ Sinton Tx
Machine work by Gilpin Engine Machine

Theo August

2003 Nissan 350z Japan import

Instagram: @theosbook

Photographer: @incogmedia

Theo is from Cape Town, South Africa and is married with two kids.

He grew up on the cape flats and had to work hard to get where he is today and more so to have the type of cars he has today.

More importantly to maintain them and ensure that they are always running and looking in the best possible condition.

What got Theo into cars was he kept seeing really nice cars on the road and he decided instead of wishing to own one of them, he decided to make it a reality.

What made Theo choose this car was when he was a youngster he always believed the Nissan 350z " sports car" was way out of his reach.

So it kind of chose him as he says… But it's funny what hard work can do, how you evolve out of wanting to be able to have.

This car just screams" sporty", this is now the 3rd 350z that he has owned, amongst owning a 2010 BMW e90 that he bought in 2010.

He also owns a 1983 Datsun Stanza. What makes this car unique to Theo in his eyes, everything, it's a 2003 import from Japan.

Everything in the car such as the Radio, GPS, cautionary stickers, labels etc are all in Japanese.

The 350z has only 84000 km on the clocks and just looks stunning and sounds louder than most. To Quote Theo

"what makes this car unique is the fact that this car is a showstopper and definitely breaks necks whenever she is on the roads".

STANCEAUTOMAG DARREN NIEUWOUDT

STANCEAUTOMAG DARREN NIEUWOUDT

Most of the work on the car was done by Leqraam and the team at Autoway in Wynberg.

Jaleel from Infinity performance did the tuning. The engine bay was done by Barry from Custom Auto Graphic. Swen from Slowys Customs did Theo`s rims and custom purge kit and most of his Nissan 350z parts came from Ahmed from VenomZworx in JHB

Future plans for the 350z include a custom rear louvre which should arrive mid-month February.

The headlights are due for a makeover and he recently got his chrome chameleon headlight, fog light vinyl smoke film and will have them fitted.

His wheels are also about to get a makeover and then he is gonna fit the long-awaited 35mm wheel spacers all around.

Venom work - 350z/ 370z & GTR

Car group are all across South Africa and he looks after the Cape Town chapter as you can see his from his car, it fully represents vZw in Cape Town.

He is also a RowdyTribe car group member (Cape Town Elite car group).

What Theo gets from the car scene is his passion for cars, not everyone is as friendly as he would've wished, lots of haters but he says it's OK.

He goes on to say "we have the guys helping each other out, sharing knowledge, offering to help fix something, give advice, donate a part here and there. Charity events and coming together is just what it's all about man".

The advice he has for new comers to the car scene and car modifying is

" Guys/Gals follow your passion It's your car and whether it be a Fiat Tata Mustang OPC Toyota it doesn't matter It's YOUR car"

" YOUR build Embrace it and pull in man, come to say hi and let's make the Cape Town car scene unique"!

STANCEAUTOMAG | DARREN NIEUWOUDT

STANCEAUTOMAG | DARREN NIEUWOUDT

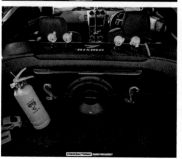

SPEC LIST

Engine:

- Cold air intake
- Custom engine cover
- Custom battery covers
- Custom tune by infinity performance
- Exhaust:
- Custom Exhaust fitted with a custom exhaust valve that can open and close at leisure

Exterior:

- Ings front bumper
- Ings side skirts
- Amuse rear bumper
- Vented bonnet
- 350z V Style trunk spoiler brought in from Canada
- Depo black Z LED tail lights from the USA
- 2x Japanese custom tow straps
- Headlight eyelids
- Customized headlights with red ` venom ' logo imprinted inside the right headlight
- 10 piece dream-chasing effect underglow car lighting
- Custom white spray job
- Blood splash and Japanese wording (Honor and Integrity) decals
- The rising sun with mountain background decals on doors

Wheels:

- 19-inch black Vossen wheels

Interior:

- Red front seats
- Paramount double din
- Custom sword style gear lever
- Amp and subwoofer

Jose David Alcantara

2009 Toyota Camry Se

Instagram: @somernp

Photographer: @villainous_media

My name is Jose David, I am 25 years old, born in Milford, Delaware but raised in Morelos, México for 10 years until I was 15 when I moved to Austin, Texas.

I am currently a supervisor for a concrete company. In my spare time, I enjoy relaxing at home playing video games or working out. I also love spending time with my friends and girlfriend or just working on my car. I love to hop in the car and just drive with no destination in mind. Something about just cruising relaxes me and is a major stress reliever.

I have always been into cars since I was a kid. My mom used to buy me a lot of toy cars and I would always paint them and make them custom. I have always enjoyed reading about cars in magazines and my room was always decorated with car posters.

When I was a kid, my favourite present ever was a Nintendo GameCube that came with the game Need for Speed Underground.

I loved that game so much that I played through it like 10 times. Another major influence for me was the fast & furious movies. Every time I watched those movies, I felt inspired to build my dream car and now I have accomplished my goal!

One night at a meet I saw this Acura TLX with a peach-coloured wrap, and I was absolutely amazed by it when the owner aired it out and it was sitting on the ground!

I decided to talk to the owner and I saw that he was part of a team that I had seen before at car shows, I asked him what the process is to join that car club, he walked over to look at my car and told me that it looked good, but I could make it look way better if I would get air suspension and get new wheels.

He told me once I got bags and some new wheels and hang out with the team, they could vote on making me a prospect and explain the full process of joining.

I am so thankful I met him and asked him about joining because now I have the greatest friends with the same passion and love that I have for cars, and they have been extremely helping me build my car to be a proper show car.

I love my car so much, it might not the fastest car or most expensive, but I really enjoy driving it and how I was able to make a Camry get so much attention from people. Anytime I park the car I spot people taking pictures of it or recording it which always brings a smile to my face.

This car truly makes me happy and really allows me to express who I am. Not many people modify older Camry's and it's often hard to find aftermarket parts for it, but I love experimenting with custom parts and it makes the build even more unique.

The reason I decided to build a Camry is that I wanted something reliable and that would save me some gas. It was not my intention to buy this car to build it nearly as far as what it has become today.

I was just looking for a car that would get me from point A to point B. I have had two Camry's already, the first one was a black 2007 which I loved but I got into an accident, and it was totalled.

When I was in search of my next car, I just could not decide on which one to buy. Eventually, I decided to buy another Camry Sport which was even better than my last one. Now I have owned the car for about 5 years.

As I said, it wasn't my intention to start building this car, but then I started to look for small stuff to put in my car to make it more personal. Honestly, I had no idea how to modify it, so I bought a lot of random stuff from Amazon and AutoZone which really taught me about what not to do to a car. It did not look good at all. I would still take the car to meets to see other people's cars and get some ideas.

The colour I chose (voodoo Blue) is my favourite colour and it came out on Toyota Tacoma's years after my car was made. What I love most about this car and modifying cars are the people I have met during this amazing journey. It has given me a new family that is always willing to help me out and so many new friends.

When people see the car in shows or car meets, it's just an amazing feeling because you can see it on their faces that they like the car. It is an honour to create a build that is loved by so many people, and I am lucky to have been blessed with so much love from people.

This car is proof that with determination and hard work you can accomplish your dreams and goals and I hope it can be an inspiration to anyone that has the same dream.

I have done a lot of work on my car but if there's something I struggle with, my friends are always down to help me out and I appreciate them!

My car would not be where it is today without their help. You know who you are, you guys are the best! I have learned so much thanks to you all!

SPEC LIST

Engine:
- Custom Headers
- K&N Air Intake

Exterior:
- Carbon Fiber Hood
- Carbon Fiber Trunk
- Carbon Fiber Duckbill
- Carbon Fiber Door Pillars
- Custom Paint Job (Voodoo Blue)
- Full Aero kit by Aeroflow Dynamics (Front splitter, Rear diffuser and Side skirts)
- Lowglow Underglow lighting
- Aftermarket Headlights
- Aftermarket Taillights

Interior:
- Carbon Fiber Steering Wheel
- Carbon Fiber Interior Pieces
- Carbon Fiber Shift Knob
- Custom headliner, pillars and trunk lid made with black suede and 1,300 starlights with two shooting stars
- Custom Floor Mats

Wheels and Tires:
- SSR Executor CV04 Wheels

With special colour faces from SSR (Spectrum Silver) and Laser engraved on the lip with the wheel series (Executor) 19x10 +11 squared
- Sumitomo tires 225, 35, 19 all around

Suspension:
- Airtek Air Suspension and Airlift 3P Management
- Viair 444C Dual Compressors

Future Plans

This is a car that I plan to keep, even if the engine breaks, I will buy a new engine for it.

In the future, I am planning of doing a custom widebody and get more carbon fibre parts, for the engine I want to get the engine cover, the radiator cover, and fuse box cover in carbon fibre. I would also like to get new seats and add more stuff to my interior and a nice trunk setup for my air ride.

Advice Tips

For anyone interested in building a Camry like my generation or any other car, I can tell you that with the right research and dedication you can make any car look great!

Just make it your own, your car is a reflection of yourself, it doesn't matter if some people don't like it, if you are happy with it, that is all that matters.

Also, take your time and be patient. It took me 4 years to make this car look the way it is right now and honestly; it has been so worth it!

Shout Outs

The team that I asked to join is "Team Diverse" and it is one of the best things that ever happened to me, being part of this team is like having a second family, we all get along with each other and their builds are amazing!

Quality over quantity! Team Diverse, Family first!

@teamdiverse

Dream Car

The car scene has given me a lot of friends and my team that is my second family!

Before being in the car scene, I did not have a lot of friends and wouldn't really go out because I didn't know a lot of people, but now, I have friends that I love being around and enjoy going through life with them!

I am very thankful for all the memories and everything they have taught me and continue to teach me.

Sebastian Trujillo

2016 Mazda 3

Instagram: @Stan_mz3

Photographer: @_apex_visualz

I'm from a small town on the border of Washington and Oregon, USA called Umatilla.

I work for Amazon web services and if I'm not in the gym or driving around in my car you can catch me outdoors fishing or hiking.

I first really got introduced to cars because I grew up watching street outlaws with my dad on Saturday mornings. I loved American muscle but as I grew older I can't say I was "Into" cars.

For sure I appreciated them but it wasn't until my senior year or a little after high school.

My best friend had a lot to do with that when he put me onto Tj hunt or when he'd let me come over and help him work on his EG civic.

He's the one who taught me how to change my first exhaust. I owe a lot to my dad and my friend because if it weren't for those Saturday mornings or those Sunday afternoons working on the civic I don't think I would have gotten into cars at all.

I've always had a love for Mazdas, but the Mazda 3 in particular. I love hatchbacks in general but the 3 always stood out to me. I didn't get into cars until after I had bought them so I didn't plan on modifying them.

I bought it back when I didn't know any better or else I would have gotten a speed3 but I don't regret buying it whatsoever.

The more I got into cars the more I wanted to modify my car. I started to discover more and more people who had my car and it turns out there is a tight-knit community of Mazda 3 lovers.

I was inspired by so many builds I had to be part of this little community.

I did start out with a few tasteless mods, but I grew to know better. It feels great owning and driving this car, I get a lot of looks.

People always want to say I should have gotten a faster car, but I don't really care what they have to say. I have plans for the future when it comes to building a fast car, I'll get there at my own pace, I love this car for everything that it is.

Every time I get out to go into a store or restaurant I always take a second look at it because honestly if your car isn't breaking your own neck. You're doing something wrong.

The best feeling is airing out in a parking lot and watching everyone turn around in confusion, or watching random kids or adults taking pictures of my car at meets. I built this car to express my own individuality and to show my own vision of what this car can be and look like.

I think the fact that I'm on bags is unique enough at least for my car in my area. There are really only a few modded gen 3, 3's in my area that I know of, there are a few more but they're a good 3 or 4-hour drive from me.

So when I'm driving around people know that it's me most of the time, not to mention Mazda's hatchbacks do a good job standing out on their body style alone.

SPEC LIST

- Injen cold air intake
- Corksport Mid-pipe to Borla axle-back exhaust.
- Wrenchmonkee air struts with airlift 3p management.
- Aodhan DS01 wheels
- Front lip
- 10 inch Memphis subwoofer.

Still, a lot more to come.

For the most part, I did everything myself except my bag installation, I had those professionally done by @Wrenchmonkee in Kennewick, WA.

I try to do everything myself so I can learn for future builds, I virtually taught myself but I did have some help from friends.

Future Plans

There's a lot I want to do with the car from wide-body and forced induction, but those I put off just because I want to do a lot more research before I decide to pull the trigger.

Unless I get a new car then I'll just go full send. I've been looking at the new AWD turbo Mazda 3. I wouldn't mind at all staying on the platform.

Advice/Tips

People are going to make fun of you for being slow, but the car is fun to drive and there are a lot of performance parts coming out for it? Don't mind someone who has someone negative to say. Envy is a sign of admiration.

Remember there are quite a few forums and Facebook groups based on Mazda 3 enthusiasts.

As I said, it's a small community and we always help each other out. Even reach out to me on Instagram and I'd be glad to answer any questions I'm pretty familiar with the platform. If you don't connect with the car. Don't buy it!!, it is all I can say

Shout Outs

A huge shout out to the Facebook group Mazda Skyactiv Tuning and modifying.

It's filled with a bunch of chill people who are always ready to answer your questions. I've always felt the Mazda 3 community be a small family.

I can say that the car scene has brought me many new friends whether local or people who just follow me on Instagram, but I'd like to say one of the biggest things is it gave me a small sense of identity, and gave me an escape.

I know it's a cliche but the car scene and my car really did get me through a lot.

Dream car

Where do I start? The first Jap import I fell in love with was the NSX so that's always been my number one second and the third I'd have to say would be a Porsche GT3 RS or a 1986 Toyota Cressida with a 2jz swap.

STANCEAUTOMAG | DARREN NIEUWOUDT

2012 C63 AMG Coupe` Black Series

Instagram: @amg_addict_sa
Photographer: @incogmedia

Allen is semi-retired and currently resides in Cape Town, South Africa, he is a Mercedes AMG fanatic/addict as you can see.

What got him into the car scene was the college he went to, all the guys had sound systems and nice cars, so he also wanted to have the same. That led him to get his own nice cars with sound systems. He owned many different cars from supercars to sports cars and then he got his Mercedes C63 AMG Black series.

Allen drives two cars- he has a 2011 ML63 AMG (10th-anniversary edition) which has the M156, 6.2L V8 motor in. He has the 2012 C63 AMG Black Series which also comes with the uprated M156 motor with modified internals (forged pistons etc).

There were 800 made worldwide and 12 for South Africa. Also, with the steering wheel on the right-hand side, only a couple of 100 were made.

As he has driven and owned many different cars in the past, Allen says and to quote him

" this is truly a track monster. It's still amazing being 10 years old and destroying many of today's high-performance cars".

The C63 AMG Coupe` Black Series is classed as " The Dark Side Of Mercedes-AMG"

SPEC LIST

Engine
- ➤ Upgraded version of the M156 6.2L N/A V8, rated 517hp (380kw) and 620 Nm torque
- ➤ Chromed twin tailpipes

Suspension
- ➤ AMG sports suspension
- ➤ AMG rear differential lock
- ➤ Three-stage ESP

Exterior
- ➤ AMG Aerodynamics package which includes:
- ➤ Carbon fibre flicks on the front apron
- ➤ Carbon fibre functionally tuned front splitter
- ➤ Fixed carbon fibre rear aerofoil with an adjustable blade
- ➤ Black diffuser insert from the SLS AMG GT3

Interior
- ➤ Two AMG sports bucket seats
- ➤ Black DINAMICA microfibre upholstery on centre panels of seats and doors
- ➤ Omission of the rear bench seat (single rear seats available as an option)
- ➤ AMG performance steering wheel in Nappa leather/ DINAMICA microfibre
- ➤ Steering wheel rim featuring flattened top and the bottom section has aluminium shift paddles
- ➤ Red seat belts
- ➤ Red contrasting top stitching on steering wheel, seats, door centre panels, armrest on doors, centre console and shift lever gait
- ➤ Three autonomous round dials which have three dimensional TFT colour display

Wheels
- ➤ AMG Track package includes:
- ➤ 255/35 R19 Dunlop Sports tyres (Front)
- ➤ 285/35 R19 Dunlop Sports tyres (Rear)
- ➤ Active rear-axle transmission cooling with the radiator in the rear apron
- ➤ Dunlop is not available anymore, so the Michelin pilot super sports are the replacements which are M01 (AMG) standard

STANCEAUTOMAG *DARREN NIEUWOUDT*

STANCEAUTOMAG *DARREN NIEUWOUDT*

CEAUTOMAG *DARREN NIEUWOUDT*

The Black series projects from Mercedes AMG are limited, unique and very rare. Allen says you must keep your eyes open because you will only see them for a few seconds.

Everything on the Mercedes is stock, straight from the AMG factory in Affalterbach Germany. He goes on to say, changing anything on the AMG will result in devaluing the rarity of the car. The C63 AMG Black series is definitely a head-turner and not something you see every day. The aggressive look and rumble of the engine and exhaust are just out of this world.

In the car scene, Allen says, It's either in your blood or not. You should give it a try by going with some mates or someone that is a petrol head and decide from there if it's for you or not. He goes on to say " to buy a car like mine is a no-brain investment.Look at shmee150- Tim and mr amg- RAZ. Why are they investing in the black series? Tim almost has all of them. If you can, get a C63 immediately. They are going to be really valuable soon if not now".

Dream car

When asked what his dream car is. He said " well this is my dream car, what is next if you own a unicorn"

But Allen would like to have the SLS Black Series parked next to the C63 Black Series

Zac Ganfield
2009 Mk2 Ford Focus RS
Ken Block WRC Conversion

Instagram: @thatgymkhanarep

Photographer: k.k photography by Katie

K.K.PHOTOGRAPHY

I am a 22-year-old lad from Somerset that's had some wild and a wide range of fast cars starting with a 335d and fully forged Astra and a Nurburgring Corsa.

I've had boosted ep3's and a 485bhp 535 Bmw and a big spec Focus ST in pink but now I have Mollie and she's got me through loads because of this care I've got for cars and this one, I've got through a mad couple of years of stress.

I have recently had heart surgery and it's got me through every hospital scare I have an amazing team of people behind me who has got me to where I am today with the car.

A huge shout out needs to go to a very good and special friend of mine Dave Evans the owner of CyFen Autos anything I couldn't do or I wasn't sure about he would jump straight in tell me how to do it, the best way to do it and then help me do it.

Whatever I do, however mental it was he would do it no complaints and next one would be to Ash Dagge and Colton Dagge at AC Detailing father and son business.

k.k photography by Katie amazing young lady with an eye for show cars.

CyFen and AC have been Amazing Dave at CyFen has transported me up and down the country week after week, day after day without hesitation getting her ready so I'm fit for shows.

Ash AC has washed my car at the latest could be 11 - 12 o'clock at night without hesitation or complain every time the car needs cleaning he will come and do it he's a top guy I'm truly thankful for my team getting me where I am today.

The reason I got into this was I seen Ken block on Top Gear with James May and then a year or so later I saw Rich Fox when he was starting out with his MK2 Ford Focus RS.

That's when I knew that was what I wanted and that was the dream to get to that stage and he is now the prestigious Fox.

That's really the reason I got into what I do now and it's been a hell of a rollercoaster. But we've done it after everyone telling me I would never get there.

I would never own the car, I would never be able to build the car, I'm not gonna say I did it alone because that's a lie but my team and I have pulled it out of the bag and we made a monster and Mollie the monster hopefully will outlive me.

I probably don't have much time left due to recent health issues but I'm sure somebody will carry the Legacy on I love her as much as I do.

The reason I chose this car was Because of Rich Fox that is the reason I chose to go with a MK2 Focus RS

I had had a pink forged pre-facelift Focus ST2 before and I love that, it wasn't quite enough, I always have that cars reg in my windscreen to show how far I've come.

K.K.PHOTOGRAPHY

I then went for a MK2 Ford Focus RS and it has been the best and the hardest challenge I'm projecting I have ever done but I wouldn't change it for the world.

The inspiration for the design came from Ken Block's Fiesta RS and his Mk3 Ford Focus RS Rally stage car it took lots of planning and lots of attempts lots of different sizes and design flaws, but eventually, we got there and it looks brilliant.

I'm really happy with it all the exterior plastics are iridescent glitter done by Bridgewater and Taunton College body and paint department with obviously the Panther black and all the extra added exterior parts are the Ken Block hooligan stars and stripes as in roof scoop.

K.K.PHOTOGRAPHY

Engine, Palum spoiler, wings, wing mirrors Wrc Vents and a number of other things.

As you can see the car is two tone so it's half and half of both designs that I really liked I couldn't decide on which one so I have just done some people don't like it but the main thing is I do and I'm really happy with the outcome.

This car is unique not just because of the Wrap, because of all the extras that go with it the big wing the Wrc Bonnet and the standard bonnet, Wrc bonnet light pod, Wrc roof scoop, Wrc wider arch's and the two-tone wheels so I have Ken blocks hoonigan alloys and I have new Rotiforms kb1 and I have fifteen52 turbo mac all in white and all wrapped in Toyo tyres R1 and fronts R888.

But the most unique thing is my Wrc rear view mirror which is a mirror the same length as my windscreen but with 5 separate mirrors all different angles and all adjustable inside the one.

Clubs/Groups I'm apart of are:

My local pub The pig and wheel where my bonnet is on the wall in their restaurant. Taylor, Dale and Tracey Stote,these are an amazing group of people that have an incredible business and a brilliant brand of auto seal and bike seals. This sealant is a unique puncture prevention system, unlike any other tyre sealant on the market. Its unrivalled technology is superior, providing a permanent prevention solution as part of safe tyre management.

Groups:

MK2 Wings, Ford Mania UK, Asbo Boyz, Nitro Nation, Southwest Focus members, Auto Cloud 9, YummyStance, Syvecs Owners Club.

The last point is about the car scene and what I get from it. It is the chance to bring lots of people together who all have a love and passion for cars which helps everyone with their own personal issues and feelings to make them more comfortable.

To help with their own mental Heath problems and issue which all together ignite that fight and passion we all have to make us stronger and better people in our groups and clubs it's pretty much a big family.

SPEC LIST

- †– I've probably missed lots but this is what I have as it stands to knowledge:
- †– WRC Ken block body Kit
- †– Iridescent millions glittered WRC MK2 Wings big wing
- †– Iridescent millions glittered WRC MK2 Wings light pods
- †– Wrc Windows
- †– Iridescent millions glittered Wrc Door Cards
- †– Full engine plastic iridescent millions glittered dress up
- †– Half cage
- †– Rich fox vide boot built with mini monster energy drinks fridge inside
- †– Revo Stage 4 software
- †– Stage 4 POP and BANG Map
- †– AIRTEC Stage 3 Intercooler
- †– AIRTEC Big Boost Pipe Kit With Red Hoses
- †– 4 x KEN BLOCK stamped fithteen52 turbo Mac
- †– 4x Ken block hoonicorn
- †– 2 x rotiform KB1 Wheels In Gloss White With Custom Graphics
- †– Toyo tyres on Toyo r888 on front 235/35/19 and toyo proxy on front
- †– 225/40/18 Tyres All Round
- †– Full custom one-off dual ram air filter cross over With Stainless Posts
- †– 3-Piece Intake Hose Kit In Red
- †– 4-Piece Pro Hose Kit In Red
- †– 5-Piece Coolant Hose Kit In Red pro hoes
- †– Upgraded Throttle Body
- †– AIRTEC Inlet Plenum In Performance hoonigan Stars & Stripes
- †– Bosch 650cc Injectors
- †– Forged Plumb Back Recirc Valve
- †– TurboSmart Actuator
- †– 3" High Flow DownPipe
- †– 3.5ich custom flame boost De-cat 6.5inch exhaust tips
- †– Carpet (Boost, Oil Pressure, Oil Temp)
- †– Bilstein coilovers all round
- †– Full bucket seats from GSM motorsport and hooligan Stars & Stripe harness
- †– Momo hooligan steering wheel quick release
- †– Hooligan Gear shifter with short shift
- †– Wrc rearview mirror

Future plans

Wider arch's and air ride and I would like to get a show truck which is fully wrapped, with modified wheels and fully airlifted, also full interior and exterior dress-up. Finnish all the iridescent millions glitter and get the cage painted, an iPad slide show centre console, and Syvecs big turbo and sidewinder build with 1000bhp with K sport braking kit and M-sport spoiler then she should be just about finished and then build her a mini-me mk7 WRC fiesta rs

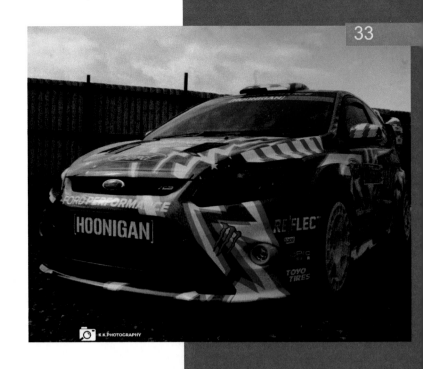

John Bowman
2001 Behrman Honda Prelude

Instagram: @Hondahots

Photographer: @trey.coleman.photos

Hi there! My name is John C. Bowman, and I am 26 years old. Coming from a military-oriented family, I have lived in Kansas, North Carolina, Oklahoma, Florida, and good ole' Tennessee which is my current home since 2010.

I specialize in High-Performance Engineering with an Associate's in Mechanical Engineering. During my period of obtaining my mechanical background, I was in a motorcycle accident that left me with an amputated limb.

This gave me a disadvantage in the automotive industry due to myself being a "high risk" employee. In 2015, I began my career journey in the tech industry with Blue Cross Blue Shield.

Over the years, my expertise has now shifted into my current role in Web Development. My side hustles tie in with my passion for cars. During my free time, you will catch me hunting for, buying, and reselling hard-to-find car parts.

Along with actively working on car projects, you can always catch me with a camera in my hand. In the past year, I have taken up photography very seriously and hope to expand on my skill even more in the upcoming months.

Outside of the realm of cars, I love to travel and experience new things with my partner-in-crime. Oh! One more thing, I love my cats.

Let's take a blast at the past. In 2005, my best friend from elementary school showed off his hot wheels and model cars to me. We would race them with homemade tracks and ramps. This is how my expensive hobby started! As time went on, I began using YouTube and online forums to teach myself how to work on cars.

What really set things into full motion was stealing my mother's 1992 25th edition purple Camaro. Yes, I did get caught, and it was so worth the butt-whooping!

Many years later, I finally was gifted the car from my parents to restore her back to its original form. I finished this restoration project in 2021 and did a Mother/Son road trip back to where the car was originally purchased, Daytona Beach, FL.

When my first car was totalled, I began searching for affordable, reliable coupes in 2012. My father saw a beautiful, white 1999 Honda Prelude for sale nearby.We checked it out, and it was the perfect fit for my tastes. As time went on and the "Fast and Furious" scene came into play, I began going all out with my eBay-built Honda!

My dream was short-lived once a teenager ploughed into me in 2017 totalling out my 1st car build.I didn't give up and soon found my replacement.I picked up my Black 2001 Honda Prelude,which is now the beautiful, blue Prelude you see today. She is known globally as "Athena".

What made you customise it?

As mentioned previously, my 1st Prelude was a true, authentic eBay-built car! With that being said, I did many things incorrectly and cut a lot of corners.

During this go-round on having a second chance to redo my choices, I decided to exceed all expectations. I touched every inch of this car from the exterior, interior, engine, and electrical. It was my goal to be one of the very few Behrman Preludes internationally.

I have always had a passion for the Honda Prelude. While this car typically goes unnoticed in the streets, I always spot them from a mile away!

STANCEAUTOMAG TREY COLEMAN

My mind always had a vision of how I wanted to interpret the Prelude, and that is exactly what I have done with Athena.

After many hours, sweat, tears, money, and hand injuries, I finally completed the build of my dreams.

Every time I am behind the wheel of my car, there is a rush of happiness running through my veins. I built this for myself, but it is an honour that my car is used as an example for many other Honda enthusiasts for their Prelude builds.

I'm proud and humbled to know Athena is catching the attention that she is all due to me having a dream.

What makes your car unique?

The definition of the Honda Prelude is "an action or event serving as an introduction to something new or more important." That is exactly what I have done with Athena. Let's start with the most eye-catching feature of the vehicle at a quick glance -- paint!

I decided to go with Dodge's Surf Blue Pearl with even more pearl than what the paint code calls for. You will also notice some 'strange' emblems on the vehicle. They are NOT standard OEM Honda emblems that can be purchased. I collaborated with MirroredAcrylics to create custom 1:1 front/rear emblems using my signature and an illuminated rear license plate.

After speaking with leadership from Wisesquare.jp, I am one of very few Honda Preludes worldwide that is driven on the roads with a complete Behrman body kit. Let's move on to the heart of Athena. Once the hood pops, you will be greeted with custom glass radiator hoses manufactured by Killerglass, a custom dimple dies window cowl created by SolKreations365, and multiple billet aluminium BBAlliance dress-up parts.

Lastly, when sitting in the driver seat of Athena, your attention will be grabbed immediately by a 1:1 LED-based gauge cluster made by XTuners Tuning Studio that features my signature and the name Athena.

SPEC LIST

Engine Bay:
- BBA radiator brackets
- BBA cooling plate
- BBA power steering delete plate
- KillerGlass glass radiator hoses
- KillerGlass radiator hose LEDs (4 green)
- KillerGlass velocity stack
- Mishimoto radiator
- Mishimoto fan shroud
- Plm ram horn headers
- Exedy Clutch
- Fidanza lightweight flywheel
- Esp alternator bracket
- Esp front torque mount
- Esp rear t bracket
- Esp motor mounts
- Mpc hundred proof engine hardware
- Mpc hundred proof transmission hardware
- Mpc block off plate
- Mpc hundred proof vc hardware
- Wilwood master cylinder
- Bwr brake booster delete plate (polished)
- Bwr billet oil cap
- Fender washers (40pc)
- Steel braided clutch line
- Spark plug spacers
- 40/40 proportioning valve (abs delete)
- Led engine bay kit
- Hood struts
- Spark plug wires (red)
- Golden eagle cam seal
- Golden eagle solenoid cover
- Rywire 61 pin connector kit
- Evolution PCV valve extension
- Weapon R radiator reservoir
- Weapon R power steering reservoir
- Powder coat valve cover purple
- Powder coat intake mani chrome
- Powder coat booster delete plate chrome
- Powder coat radiator brackets chrome
- Powder coat cooling plate chrome
- Shaving engine bay
- VMS header bolts
- K-tuned engine ground wires
- Silicone radiator hose kit

Suspension:

- SPC rear camber kit
- T1r 2.0 neo chrome lug nuts
- Air Lift 3p management
- Air Lift 3h upgrade kit
- D2 struts/bags
- Custom shortened lower control arms
- St sway bars
- St sway bar bushings
- Esp traction bar system
- Drilled and slotted rotors
- Mpc drop forks
- Wheels:
- Work Meisters S1 3P 18x10 +43
- Audio:
- Atoto radio
- Polk audio speakers front w/ crossovers
- Kicker rear speakers
- 12" Rockford phosgate sub

Interior:

- Honda access door sills
- Honda access carbon fibre trim
- Honda access auto headlights
- Honda access security system
- Honda access fog light switch w/ bezel
- Honda access rear sunshade usdm
- Jdm cup holder
- Jdm digital climate control
- Jdm rear ashtray
- Jdm cig outlet
- Jdm ashtray
- Honda access chrome ring bezel
- Edm gauge speedo
- Edm red door lights
- Type s red-stitched seats
- Type sh door panels (black)
- Type sh rear deck
- JTC short shifter
- Nardi steering wheel 350mm
- Nardi steering wheel cover
- Nardi prestige line perforated leather knob
- Nardi leather shift boot
- Nardi Leather hand brake boot
- Nrg hub
- Nrg quick release
- Nrg quick-lock hub
- Spoon blue wide rearview mirror
- Integra rearview mirror

Exterior:

- Honda access fog lights jdm style
- Honda access hood spoiler
- Honda access car cover w/ bag
- Honda access yellow covex mirrors
- Honda access gunmetal grey grill
- Jdm fenders
- Jdm bumper support
- Jdm clear side markers
- Type s flush mount spoiler
- Type s grill emblem
- Type s rear badge
- Prelude vanity plate
- Behrman front bumper
- Behrman side skirts
- Behrman rear bumper
- WeatherTech window visors
- Retrofitted headlights
- Repainted b5 blue
- Magnaflow muffler #14816
- Ebay clear taillights
- Led headlight bulbs
- Led 2 in 1 fog bulbs
- Window tint 20% and 70% ceramic front
- Prelude Nation front window banner
- Stature banner
- Xkglow devil eye kit
- Xkglow devil eye extension harness
- Powder coat callipers neon yellow
- Mirrored acrylic indiglow emblems

I'd like to start this section off by shouting out Teddy Gibson, the painter of Athena.

He drove many times (5+ hours) to teach me how to dismantle, prep, paint, and buff my Honda Prelude. Not many know, but the car was painted in my basement, and he worked his magic to ensure an A+ paint job was done.

The second person I'd like to shout out is myself. I completed the following tasks with no assistance: Installing Air Ride Suspension, Full Engine bay tuck, Reassembling the drivetrain, Interior swap, and obtaining all rare goodies for the car.

The third and final shout out goes to Middle Tennessee Fab & Performance with always lending a hand in all my car builds. They assisted with completing a motor swap in a time crunch and all my typical maintenance needs. MTFP will be the shop that completes the Height Sensor install, Trunk setup, and the Jackson Racing Supercharger build.

Advice/Tips

The very first thing that anyone should look out for when purchasing an older Honda is rust. If you buy a northern Honda, always check to make sure there is NO RUST. Dealing with this causes more headache, money, and time than what it's worth. Don't do it!

The second thing I suggest is always pulling a Carfax. I cannot tell you how many times I have come across clocked odometers. It is a thing, and it can happen to you. Don't allow yourself to be taken advantage of!

The third thing that is a common occurrence in the 5th generation Honda Prelude is that automatic transmissions are notorious for going bad. So let's go ahead and make sure you have a spare off to the side or stick with a 5 speed!

Future Plans

The next big project that I will be tackling is boosting the car with a Jackson Racing Supercharger for the H22; however, that is going to be the last thing on my wishlist. Currently, I have two other projects I must tend to at this given time.

Shout Outs

Stature - @StatureCrew.tm
Slammedenuff - @Slammedenuff
Battlegang - @Battlegvng.tm
BBAlliance TB - @BBAlliancetb
StreetLab - @_StreetLab
Middle Tennessee Fab and Performance - @mtfp_built

The car scene has moulded my life to where it is today. I will forever be thankful for the unforgettable experiences and memories that have occurred up to this point.Car brands hosting shows all across the USA has allowed me, my friends, and my family to travel for more than just leisure.

It has provided opportunities to showcase our passion with others! I look forward to future events and cannot wait to see where history takes us next.

Ethan Herman

2012 Subaru Impreza WRX STI

Instagram: @Ethan_herman6

I'm a new Nashville resident. I was a project manager for a remediation company and have just gone back to school at MTSU for a construction management degree.

My dad and my older brother got me into the car scene. It was a bond for all of us.

None of us ever had the best relationship but cars were something we all had in common to talk about.

I drive a 2012 Subaru Impreza WRX STI and a 2019 Chrysler 300S and I also have a 2008 Harley 1200.

All of these vehicles have their own particular reasons why I chose them. I decided to build this car because it had lots of potentials and just needed some love. I have a thing for unique looking cars and mine is definitely not one you see very often.

Having people look at you while you driving or waving or giving a thumbs up when they're going the other way has to be one of the best feelings in the world.

It will never get old. Personally, I've had no issues with the car since I've had it. It has super low miles and even with all the modifications, there haven't been any issues with the car or its driving.

I'm a very firm believer in the fact that everyone has their own individual taste when it comes to cars and that includes modifications.

The only advice I have is to modify your car however you want and however you can afford it. At the end of the day, you are the one who has to drive the car home so if you like it, who cares.

Most of the work I have not done myself. I wish I had the time to but between working full time and now going to school full time along with all my other responsibilities, it's not very practical.

I figured I would rather enjoy the car than let it sit. As of now, I don't have any future plans for the car. Possibly I'll put it on air suspension so I don't scrape the front lip all over the place but scraping is part of the enjoyment of the car.

Since I recently moved to Nashville I joined a Facebook group called Nashville Subaru's, It's a great community and the meets at Cars and Coffee on the first Saturday of every month are the best. Everyone in the group is helpful, extremely friendly and very welcoming.

The car scene has brought me countless great memories and friends throughout the years.

Whether it was hanging out with the old guys at the meets when my dad and I bought our first project car, a 71 beetle convertible, or meeting my brother's friends through his meets.

What makes my car unique is the colour, It was originally the factory silver from Subaru but it needed a bit of a change so it got wrapped in the Satin Desert Storm Tan vinyl wrap.

SPEC LIST

Performance:
- †– K&N Typhoon Short Ram Intake,
- †– HKS Hipermax IV GT Coilovers,
- †– Invidia R400 Gemini Titanium catback exhaust,
- †– Cobb v3 accessport,
- †– Cusco rear lower control arms.

Exterior:
- †– MntRider Design Widebody kit.

Interior:
- †– STI Alcantara seats.

Wheels:
- †– Cosmis Racing XT206R 20x11.

Tires:
- †– 315/30R/20 Toyo R888r

Eric Strickland

1995 NISSAN SKYLINE BCNR33

Instagram: @okiegtr
Photographer: Adam Delgadillo - @oadam7
Photographer: Seth Fox - @ulphotog
Location: Oklahoma

I've been building cars since the late 80s. I believe that form, function, and fashion can exists together.

Why did you choose this vehicle/ platform?

The Skyline platform has always intrigued me since the early 2000s. While the R34 was the version everyone drooled over, the R33 is what caught my eye.

At that point in time, I never thought I would be lucky enough to own an R33 GTR, much less one built to this specification.

Do you have any prior build experience?

Yes, I have built a few vehicles over the years. My obsession started just towards the end of high school. I was already into car audio and doing some local car shows.

This was back in the times of mini-trucks and booming systems. In the mid-90s I switched over to the IMPORT scene.

The car was a 1994 Honda Accord 4 door EX. My main goal was to replicate the Accord SiR from Japan. This car turned into a turbocharged beast sporting just under 400 whp, which was a foot back in the late 90s.

That car was sold to a gentleman back east. Then came the introduction of the Subaru WRX and I could not keep away. Purchased a 2002 Rally Blue in mid-October and instantly went to work to replicate the WRC rally car. Everything from the roof vent & scoop to the overly huge WRC rear spoiler. This car went through many phases over its 6 years of ownership and was finally sold to a gentleman in Norway.

What got you into building in the first place?

A friend from college and his girlfriend, now wife. Her parents had a show car and they toured in a series with the Auto-Rama, World of Wheels, etc events.

The big indoor stuff. I started doing some smaller shows with them and they showed me how to properly clean and display a vehicle to not only compete, but to win at the indoor shows. I was pretty hooked from that point on.

What is your favourite aspect of the build?

This all started back in 2008 when I received the car. I already had a plan of attack and the overall look I wanted. Was I going to achieve that plan??? At time who knew. The best aspect of this build has been definitely learning where to source parts, who to trust, and also helping others along the way that we're pursuing the same goals.

Were there any major challenges you experienced in the build?

The main challenges were simply trying to come up with the sources to get parts. Back in the earlier days of the Skylines being around.

Sourcing parts was a nightmare at first, until you figured out who in the states was legit at getting parts as well as getting the best prices, not only in the states but also abroad. Once these issues were resolved, life became better.

Much of the information obtained was from some Skyline friends down in the Dallas, TX area. Those guys are the best. The other way to overcome building a Skyline is the have the "Fat Wallet Mod 11, because you will need it.

What were your original intentions with the build?

Original goals were to build an "all-around" car. Be able to take it to car shows and discuss with people of all ages about the car, as well as take it to a road course and beat on her some. Which I have done. The only changes that have taken place are when new/ old parts that I originally wanted have become available.

Why did you choose certain brands for your build?

When I received the car back in early 2008, I called Brice at Alamo Autosports in Arlington, Texas and told him what I had just done.

He had already built a Honda and a Subaru for me over the years. I asked him his opinion between GReddy/Trust & HKS and he said at the time GReddy/Trust had more parts available.

So we placed an order from GReddy and it was at Alamo in 2 weeks. That is when it all started.

The RB Shop out in New Jersey was also a huge help during the rebuild stages of the motor, lots of great information & input.

Michael Ferrara at Club DSport did a fabulous job on the head, explaining all phases and sending images throughout'

What influences or inspiration helped you over the course of your build?

First and foremost, definitely Brice Yingling at Alamo Autosports. He was able to answer questions and suggest ways to achieve my goals.

The original North Texas Skyline guys were also a huge help. Can't forget my group of friends over the years that have helped, especially during the 26-month restoration.

Is there anything about the build experiences, that you would like readers to know?

First and foremost, make a plan of attack. Know what your goals are. Set them high, but not out-of-the-world high.

Have a financial budget set and "try" to keep to it. Always remember, Rome was not built in 1 year.

Interesting facts about your build:

Just a couple of parts that are, "to the best of my knowledge" the only ones like them in the USA.

The engraved Cusco titanium front strut bar (very rare), Stout.JP carbon hood, 400R carbon lip spoiler, and the AutoSelect Devil Wing.

I also want to thank Brice at Alamo Autosports in Arlington, Texas & '1Lastlega1Skyline' at the RBShop for all the assistance and knowledge during this build.

Without them, this build would not be to the calibre it is.

Special thanks to:

Brice Yingling
@AlamoAutosports

Andy Dennington
@1UpFabrication

John Manett
@ManettsMegaShine

SPEC LIST

Engine:

- Nissan RB26 0SU Block
- Tomei Oil Pump
- Supertec Racing Spline Drive
- Tomei 272 x 10.15 ProCams
- Tomei Cam Cap Studs
- GReddy Adjustable Cam Gears
- GReddy Kevlar Timing Belt
- NISMO Nl Water Pump
- NISMO Oil Pan Baffle
- NISMO Gasket Set
- Supertech Valves
- Supertech Titanium Retainers
- Supertech Dual Valve Springs
- Supertech Guides & Seats
- Manley "H" Beam Rods
- Wiseco 86.5mm Pistons - 9.1 :1
- Cosworth 1.1 mm Head Gasket
- ARP Studs & Bolts Throughout
- Garrett GT 2860-S+B Turbos
- HKS Actuators
- ATI Harmonic Balancer
- GKTech Hi-Flow Fan
- ACL Race Bearings
- AEM H2O-CH3OH Kit
- Apex-i SS Downpipe
- Tomei Expreme Manifolds
- Tomei Outlet Pipes
- 1 UP Fab Hard Pipes
- 1 UP Fab Suction Kit

Performance:

- GReddy 90mm Surge Tank
- GReddy Type 29 FMIC
- GReddy Airinx Filters
- GReddy Oil Filter Relocator
- GReddy Oil Cooler
- GReddy Aluminum Radiator
- GReddy 1.3 Bar Radiator Cap
- GReddy Water/ Air Separator
- GReddy Pulley Kit
- GReddy Front & Rear Diff Covers
- NISMO Oil Cap
- NISMO Low Temp Thermostat
- 1-Up Fab Twin 65mm Exhaust
- 1-Up Fab Suction Kit
- 1-Up Fab IC Hard Pipes
- 1-Up Fab Upper Radiator Pipe
- 1-UP Fab Oil Separator
- 1-UP Fab Coolant Overflow
- Mine's Camshaft Baffle
- Alamo Super Custom 11 mm Fuel Rail
- Deatschwerks 1000 cc Injectors
- Deatschwerks DW400 Fuel Pump x 2
- Deatschwerks Fuel Pressure Reg
- Fragola P.T.F.E. Fuel Lines
- NISMO Super Copperplate Twin Clutch
- NISMO Chromoly Flywheel
- GKTech Stainless Clutch Line
- Tial 42mm BOV
- Supertec Racing R35 Adapter Plates
- Hitachi R35 Coil Packs
- Silk Road Torque Dampner
- SAMCO Heater & Radiator Hose
- NISMO Rear Diff Cooler
- DriveShaft Shop 1 pc AL Driveshaft

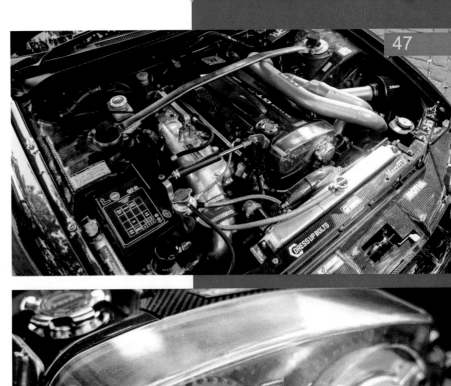

Interior:
- NISMO Rear Floor Mats
- NISMO Gauge Cluster
- NISMO Aux Gauge Cluster
- NISMO Leather Shift Knob
- GReddy A-Pillar Gauge Pod
- BRIDE Front Floor Mats
- Sparco 4-Point Harness
- Sparco Harness Bar

Carbon Fiber Trim Pieces:
- East Bear 3 Gauge Center Pod
- 5th Element Carbon Trunk Wall
- Custom Factory Bucket Seats
- R34 Momo Steering Wheel

Dress Up:
- Nissan R35 GTR Rear Badge
- Nissan R34 GTR Engine Cover
- NISMO Carbon B-Pillar Trim
- NISMO Carbon Bonnet Lip
- Hella Super Tone Horns
- Garage Defend Carbon Cooling Panel
- EP Racing Carbon Fuse Box Cover
- EP Racing Carbon Grill
- Custom Coil Pack Cover
- Dress Up Bolts
- Titanium Fasteners
- GReddy Clear Front Cover

Electronics:
- ATOTO A6 Pro Android Media Center
- Kicker QS 6.75" Mids & Tweeters
- Kicker LS 1 0" Woofer
- Kicker IQ 1000.5 Amplifier
- XM Satellite Radio
- AEM Air - Fuel Gauge
- Defi BF Series Gauges (5)
- ATS Turbo Timer
- GReddy Dampner Controller
- AEM Cam Trigger Disc
- MAXX ECU Race ECU

Dress Up:
- Nissan R35 GTR Rear Badge
- Nissan R34 GTR Engine Cover
- NISMO Carbon B-Pillar Trim
- NISMO Carbon Bonnet Lip
- Hella Super Tone Horns
- Garage Defend Carbon Cooling Panel
- EP Racing Carbon Fuse Box Cover
- EP Racing Carbon Grill
- Custom Coil Pack Cover
- Dress Up Bolts
- Titanium Fasteners
- GReddy Clear Front Cover

Electronics:
- ATOTO A6 Pro Android Media Center
- Kicker QS 6.75" Mids & Tweeters
- Kicker LS 1 0" Woofer
- Kicker IQ 1000.5 Amplifier
- XM Satellite Radio
- AEM Air - Fuel Gauge
- Defi BF Series Gauges (5)
- ATS Turbo Timer
- GReddy Dampner Controller
- AEM Cam Trigger Disc
- MAXX ECU Race ECU

Exterior:
Paint - Midnight Purple II LV4 (R34 Color)
- NISMO 400R Front Bumper
- NISMO 400R Carbon Front Splitter
- NISMO 400R Side Skirts
- NISMO Rear Spats
- NISMO Smoked Side Markers
- NISMO Clear Turn Signals
- STOUT Type-R Carbon Hood
- Garage Defend Carbon Canards
- Ganador Carbon Mirrors
- East Bear LED Tail Lamps
- Bee Racing Carbon Side Diffusers
- Top Secret Carbon Rear Diffuser
- Top Secret Carbon Vortex Generators
- Maxton Designs Cab Spoiler
- AutoSelect Carbon Devil Wing

Interior:
- NISMO Rear Floor Mats
- NISMO Gauge Cluster
- NISMO Aux Gauge Cluster
- NISMO Leather Shift Knob
- GReddy A-Pillar Gauge Pod
- BRIDE Front Floor Mats
- Sparco 4-Point Harness
- Sparco Harness Bar

Carbon Fiber Trim Pieces:
- East Bear 3 Gauge Center Pod
- 5th Element Carbon Trunk Wall
- Custom Factory Bucket Seats
- R34 Momo Steering Wheel

Suspension:
- GReddy Type "S" Coilovers
- NISMO Anti-Sway Bars
- NISMO Rear 4-Link Brace
- NISMO Rear Circuit Link Set
- NISMO Rear Lower A-Arm
- NISMO Front Tension Rods
- NISMO Front Circuit Link Set
- NISMO Motor Mounts
- NISMO Transmission Mount
- NISMO Center Reinforcing Bars
- NISMO R34 Trunk Floor Brace
- CUSCO Tension Rod Brace
- CUSCO Titanium Strut Bar - 1.27 Lbs
- CUSCO Rear AL Strut Bar
- Final Motion Carbon Air Guides
- Ultra Racing Sub Frame Braces
- Nagisa Auto Gacchiri Fender Brace
- Driftworks HICAS Eliminator Kit
- Custom Carbon Reinforcement
- KTS Roll Center Adapter
- Whiteline Sway Bar Endlinks
- Whiteline Sub Frame Bushings
- Whiteline & SuperPro Bushings

Rollers & Stoppers:
- Desmond EVO II 18 x 10.5 + 15
- Nitto 555 G2 - 285/35-18
- Rotora 6 pot Calipers (F)
- Rotora 14" Rotors (F)
- Rotora 4 pot Calipers (R)
- Rotora 13.5" Rotors (R)
- Rotora Stainless Brake Lines
- CUSCO Master Cylinder Brace
- KICS Racing Titanium Lug Nuts
- GKTech ABS Delete

Jack McKenna

2010 BMW 335i E92

Instagram: @Messing_e92

I'm 24 years old, originally from Liverpool, England but now living my best life in Gold Coast Australia.

I am a special class fitter working in the oil and gas industry. My dream as a young boy was to own a car like this and that dream came true just under a week ago when I bought this amazing 335i. Even though it was my dream I never actually thought it would come true.

The car in my short time of owning it is extremely quick. Off the mark for its age it is amazing. The interior is classy, comfy and just a joy to be in.

There's not a lot of cars in this price range that can really top this car, especially this one with the options it has which is so much more than you need.

The car to me is one of a kind, especially the model in this colour which is messing metallic. From my research, this is the only 335i in messing metallic in the world. So I haven't done any to it myself but in the near future, I intend to do a lot.

It has a multimedia entertainment system. It has power steering, data dots, cruise control and LED headlamps. This BMW 3 Series has remote central locking. This car has climate control air conditioning. Using the multi-function steering wheel, listen to your favourite music and answer calls without taking your hands off the wheel.

I've never gotten lost with the inbuilt GPS navigation system. Last but not least this car has voice recognition, keyless start, 19" alloy wheels, Bluetooth functionality, USB audio input and a proximity key with central locking.

PERFORMANCE:

So this 335i is stock with an in-line 6 cylinder twin-turbo N54 engine.

It sits at around 300hp and 400NM of torque. The average 0-100 is around 5.5 seconds

Engine Type:
- Piston Engine Size (cc): 2979 cc
- Engine Size (L) 3.0 L
- Induction:
- Turbo Intercooled
- Engine Configuration:
- In-line Cylinders: 6
- Power:
- 225kW @ 5800 rpm
- Torque:
- 400 Nm @ 1200-5000rpm
- Power to Weight Ratio:
- 150.0 kW/t
- Acceleration 0-100km/h: 5.4 s

Our Photographers

Darren Nieuwoudt

Photographer/ Author

Instagram:
@incogmedia
Facebook Page:
@incogmedia

Adam Delgadillo

Photographer/Author

Instagram: @oadam7
Facebook: Adam
Delgadillo Photography

John Hoholik

Photographer/ Author

Instagram
@buckys_photography

Antonio Logan

Photographer/Author

Instagram:
*@logan_photography_*

Donnie Roc
Photographer/Author

www.r0cean11.com
www.Facebook.com/r0cean11
www.Instagram.com/r0cean11

Photography for me started as a hobby. I have been practising for a little over 15 years now. I was building cars for SEMA before I really dove into the world of automotive photography. I shot mainly for myself as it was and still remains a passion. I did not really get serious until the last car I built was totalled.

I now shoot and write for not only Stance Auto Magazine; I also shoot for PASMAG, Official Racewars USA, Just Vibes Events, and am now affiliated with R1 Concepts. I cover many other events around the United States as well. Automotive photography for me is a way to capture not just a car but the story behind the car. Each builder puts a part of themselves into their cars. As a photographer, it's my job to tell that story and share it through my lens.

You can check out my Facebook page for all my events coverage along with many individual car shoots I have done.

Feel free to reach out with questions!

CJ Gutierrez
2005 S2000

Instagram: @c_gootrez

Photographer: @6spd_media

Next Months Feature Car

STANCEAUTOMAG | ANDRE UNGARO

	Monday	Tuesday	Wednesday	Thursday	Friday	Saturday	Sunday
APR IL 2022	28	29	30	31	1	2	3
	4	5	6	7	8	9	10
	11	12	13	14	15	16	17
	18	19	20	21	22	23	24
	25	26	27	28	29	30	1

Made in United States
Orlando, FL
22 May 2022